Harvesters

Lori Dittmer

CREATIVE EDUCATION
CREATIVE PAPERBACKS

seedlings

Published by Creative Education and Creative Paperbacks
P.O. Box 227, Mankato, Minnesota 56002
Creative Education and Creative Paperbacks
are imprints of The Creative Company
www.thecreativecompany.us

Design by Ellen Huber; production by Joe Kahnke
Art direction by Rita Marshall
Printed in the United States of America

Photographs by Alamy (All Canada Photos, John Eccles, Edwin Remsberg, Tim Scrivener), Getty Images (Fuse, Blaine Harrington III), iStockphoto (BanksPhotos, holicow, i-Stockr, kamski, stefann11), Shutterstock (Fotokostic, Lemusique, Martin Lisner, stefan11, Matthew J Thomas, tlorna, Volosina)

Library of Congress Cataloging-in-Publication Data
Names: Dittmer, Lori, author.
Title: Harvesters / Lori Dittmer.
Series: Seedlings.
Includes bibliographical references and index.
Summary: A kindergarten-level introduction to harvesters, covering their purpose, parts, role in farming, and such defining features as their headers.
Identifiers: ISBN 978-1-60818-909-0 (hardcover) / ISBN 978-1-62832-525-6 (pbk) / ISBN 978-1-56660-961-6 (eBook)
This title has been submitted for CIP processing under LCCN 2017940113.

CCSS: RI.K.1, 2, 3, 4, 5, 6, 7;
RI.1.1, 2, 3, 4, 5, 6, 7; RF.K.1, 3; RF.1.1

First Edition HC 9 8 7 6 5 4 3 2 1
First Edition PBK 9 8 7 6 5 4 3 2 1

TABLE OF CONTENTS

Hello, harvesters!

Harvesters are farm machines. They are also called combines. They do three jobs.

A harvester gathers grain **crops**.

Grains are seeds used for food. They come from plants like wheat.

The driver sits in the cab. A wide header is close to the ground. It pulls up plants.

Plants move through the machine. Metal bars shake them.

This gets rid of the straw.

A blast of air cleans the seeds. Then the grain drops into a bin behind the cab.

Harvesters pull up plants. They shoot out straw and chaff.

They pour grain into a bin.

Goodbye,

harvesters!

Picture a Harvester

mirror
cab
cutter bar

header

Words to Know

chaff: seed coverings that are removed when grain is cleaned; they cannot be eaten

crops: plants that are grown for people or animals to eat and use

straw: the stems of grain plants

Read More

Dufek, Holly. *Combines.*
Austin, Tex.: Octane Press, 2015.

Maimone, S. M. *Harvesters.*
New York: Gareth Stevens, 2016.

Websites

Kids Farm
http://www.kidsfarm.com/wheredo.htm
Learn about farm equipment and animals from a farm in Colorado.

Tractors for Kids – Learn Farm Vehicles and Equipment with Blippi
https://www.youtube.com/watch?v=ZyEnVLPhjUc
Watch a video to learn more about farm machines.

Index